The Civil War

1850–1876

SADDLEBACK
EDUCATIONAL PUBLISHING

Saddleback's *Graphic American History*

SADDLEBACK
EDUCATIONAL PUBLISHING
Three Watson
Irvine, CA 92618-2767
Website: www.sdlback.com

ISBN-13: 978-1-59905-362-2
ISBN-10: 1-59905-362-4
eBook: 978-1-60291-690-6

Printed in China

12 11 10 09 08 9 8 7 6 5 4 3 2 1

One cold January night in the 1850s people crowded into Boston's Faneuil Hall to hear a talk by the famous orator Wendell Phillips.

Ralph Waldo Emerson, the well-known writer, was chairman.

And now may I present Mr. Wendell Phillips.

My friends, may I describe to you a recent happening? In Kentucky, the owner of a large plantation has died. His 500 slaves are to be sold. Imagine, if you will, a slave auction block.

The auctioneer with his black whip shows the unhappy slaves as if they were animals.

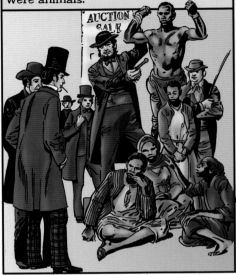

He shows the condition of their teeth, and tells their age and weight.

An interested buyer might examine his back for lash marks. Signs of too many beatings would show that the slave was a troublemaker.

Each slave goes to the highest bidder. Families are broken up, regardless of their pleas.

Sold "down the river," the slaves are shackled and marched away.

And what is the life that awaits these poor enslaved Africans on the cotton plantation down the river?

Picture the owner's beautiful mansion and the row of small earthen-floored cabins behind. Food is provided—perhaps a quart of cornmeal and a pound of salt pork a day. The cheapest clothing. Shoes for the winter months only.

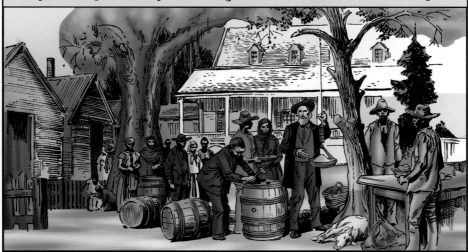

For this the slave works from sun up to sun down at his master's bidding his whole life through—unless, like lifeless property, he is sold once again.

Mr. Phillips concluded his talk. There was great applause.

The meeting was opened for discussion. A cotton mill owner arose.

Mr. Phillips exaggerates. The Southerners are not monsters. I have visited many plantations and the blacks are well-housed and well-fed. They have their own garden patches!

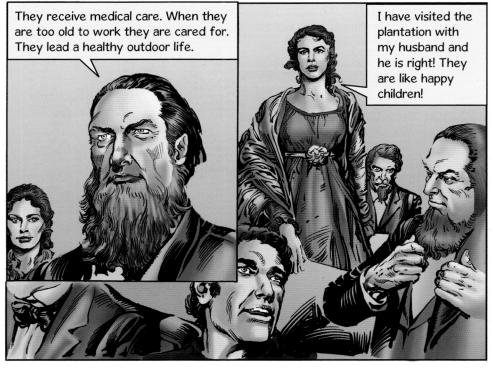

They receive medical care. When they are too old to work they are cared for. They lead a healthy outdoor life.

I have visited the plantation with my husband and he is right! They are like happy children!

And yet, ma'am, these "happy children" run away. They have been known to revolt!

It is not a matter of how well or how ill the slaves are treated. It is the fact that they are human beings!

He is God's image in ebony! No man has the right to own his life and his soul!

The more the abolitionist argued against slavery, the more the South argued in its favor.

Slavery is in conformity with the laws of the Creator. The slave is ordained to serve by the curse against Cain!

It had long been the custom for the sons of the Southern aristocracy to go north to college. Some came home with disturbing ideas.

If your professor talked abolitionist nonsense, John, don't let me hear any of it around here! Our people are happy!

But father, if the slaves are so happy, why do they run away?

Oh, John!

Those are only a few troublemakers!

Even John would not mention the secret fear of many Southerners, the slave revolts. Probably as many as 200 slave uprisings took place during the years that slavery existed. Few won freedom for any slaves, but they showed that all blacks did not accept their conditions without protest. One of the largest, in Virginia in 1831, was led by Nat Turner.

Turner learned to read and write despite laws that prohibited slaves from doing so. Studying the Bible he came to believe that he had a divine mission.

From a great black cloud an angel leaned out, telling me what I must do!

Lord! Lord!

Over a period of time, he made his plans.

Each place we go along this road, we pick up horses and arms!

There are 10,000 blacks in this country. Once we start, thousands will join us! Before the whites are alarmed, we'll reach town and seize the arsenal!

The appointed night arrived.

Let the angel of the Lord chase them. Now let us commence the battle!

What do you think you're doing in here?

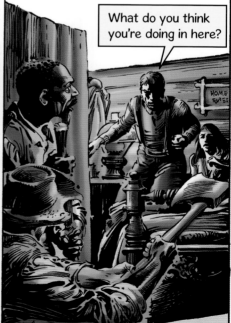

From house to house they went, leaving many dead behind them—57 in all.

Daylight came, but not the uprising of black slaves Turner had expected.

Where's that multitude supposed to join us? Ain't more than 75 of us at most!

Wait! They'll come!

But they did not come. And though state and federal troops captured Turner and his men, it was the blacks fighting to protect their masters who actually defeated them.

That's the spirit! Fire away, lads!

Look at those slaves shootin' at us!

A sometimes more successful way of winning freedom was by running away.

Traveling at night through swamps to throw off the hounds, Micah made his way.

I can't stand it no longer! I'm gonna run away!

If you can get far enough, Micah, there're free people, black and white, who'll help you.

Don't know where I am ... but they say if I follow the North Star it leads to freedom.

But slaves were valuable property. When he was missed in the morning, a search was organized.

Don't worry, sir! We'll have him back in no time.

I'm counting on you, Sheriff!

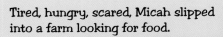

Tired, hungry, scared, Micah slipped into a farm looking for food.

Young man! Are you a runaway slave?

Oh, no, ma'am I just ... I ...

Don't argue! Just get inside here. I can hear the dogs baying behind you!

Not knowing quite how it happened, Micah found himself pushed down stairs into a musty cellar.

Just keep quiet. Not a sound!

The woman pulled a braided rug over the door, then her spinning wheel.

There!

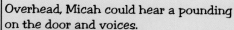

Micah heard hoofbeats going away. Then the trapdoor opened.

It is all right! They've gone. You'd best stay there to be safe, but I'll get you some food.

There's a blanket bed in the corner— try to rest. There'll be someone here tonight to take you farther.

Ma'am ... I don't rightly know how to thank you.

After dark, a mule cart full of hay stopped in front of the farmhouse.

Get in son, and burrow yourself down under that hay!

Goodbye, and God keep you!

Over empty backroads, the mule plodded along.

I'm mighty grateful ... but I wish I knew what was happenin'.

I reckon you're just lucky you stumbled into a station on the underground railroad.

If you'll excuse me—it's a mighty funny railroad.

They're like you. There's over 3,000 people running it, black and white together. The stations are places where runaway slaves can be hid. The passengers...

The conductors—they're like me! We've taken more than 100,000 slaves out of the South to freedom!

If you don't mind me asking, ma'am—were you a slave?

All my life till I ran away. Now I help others.

Reckon they should call you Moses leading your people out of slavery to the promised land!

This was Harriet Tubman, one of the most famous conductors on the underground railroad. Between 1850 and 1860, she went into the South 19 times and brought out 300 passengers. The slave owners offered a reward of $40,000 for her, alive or dead. She could say of herself: On my underground railroad I never ran my train off the track and I never lost a passenger.

In 1838, a slave named Frederick Bailey ran away. Disguised as a sailor, he went by train to Massachusetts.

May I ask your name, sir?

It's Frederick... uh...Douglass.

And I suppose you are going to the port of New Bedford. Well, God keep you, Frederick Douglass!

Thank you, sir!

Given Douglass's training in the shipyards of Baltimore, it is not surprising that he settled in the whaling port of New Bedford, a popular destination for runaway slaves.

Douglass got a job in a shipyard. In secret he had taught himself to read. Now he could read openly.

The *Liberator,* is that a good paper?

It's a fine paper—if you believe the slaves ought to be freed!

It's published by William Lloyd Garrison, a leading abolitionist. Take it and read it.

Thank you, I will!

Reading the *Liberator,* he became a great admirer of Garrison. He also began to speak against slavery himself in church meeting halls.

A good speech, Mr. Douglass!

Thank you.

Here is someone who wants to meet you, Mr. Douglass. William Lloyd Garrison!

Mr. Garrison, it's a great privilege to meet you!

You've a fine voice, sir, and you put things most intelligently. I would like you to join me on a speaking tour.

Douglass and Garrison became friends and fellow workers against slavery. They spoke to audiences throughout the North and West.

Later Douglass published his own newspaper devoted to the cause of freedom.

We're nearly ready to print. What have you decided about a name?

My paper will be called the *North Star*—pointing the way to freedom.

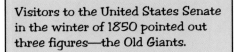

Visitors to the United States Senate in the winter of 1850 pointed out three figures—the Old Giants.

There he is—Daniel Webster, senator from Massachusetts.

America's greatest orator.

Yes ... "Liberty and Union—now and forever!" He puts saving the Union above all.

Not all of his people feel so. Some would end slavery even if it means breaking the Union.

And over there, see? Senator Calhoun from South Carolina!

Poor thing, they say he is dying but he won't give up. I admire his courage but not his ideas.

Yes, he'll fight to the bitter end for the right of the southern states to decide things for themselves.

And for the right to secede from the Union if that is the only way!

Look, Kentucky's Henry Clay! Seventy-three years old and so feeble ... but he is the buffer between the North and the South.

If he can work out an agreement this time, he will indeed be the "Great Compromiser."

What a problem it is! The western lands want to enter the Union as states, but the South won't let them enter as free states and the North won't let them enter as slave states!

The Compromise of 1850 was worked out by which California entered the Union as a free state; the settlers of the Utah and New Mexico territories could settle the question for themselves; and a new Fugitive Slave Law would make it easier for slave owners to recapture runaway slaves.

The North will hate the slave law—but without it the South would never have agreed.

Daniel, I think we have to save the Union—and end the bitter debate over slavery.

Among the people who hated the new slave law was Abe Lincoln in Illinois.

I hate to see the slaves hunted down and caught, but I bite my tongue and keep quiet.

Someday he would do more.

As it turned out the Compromise did not settle anything. It and later legislation only made the bitter debate more bitter.

In 1854, in the little frontier settlement of Ripon, Wisconsin, Major Alvin Bovay called a meeting.

The Democrats and the Whigs, the two major political parties, have northern and southern members both.

The leaders are against slavery, but they are afraid to take a stand—afraid of splitting the parties, afraid of splitting the country!

I see only one way to end the spread of slavery—form a new party, to unite all those opposed to it!

Similar meetings were held in other parts of the North.

Let us form a new party to keep slavery out of the territories! We will call ourselves Republicans!

No slavery in the territories. Join the Republican Party!

In 1854 these groups got together in a formal convention and the Republican Party was officially born.

John Brown was a New England Puritan. He believed he was ordained by God to free the slaves. Raising money from wealthy abolitionist friends, he bought a farm near Harpers Ferry, Virginia.

Only to his sons did he tell details of his plan.

> We will set up a stronghold in Virginia ... free the nearby slaves and arm them with those who join us. We will make raids throughout the South until all are free.

> But Pa, there are so few of us. Will the slaves revolt?

> Certainly, God has decreed it!

On the night of October 18, 1859, a wagon crossed the bridge to Harpers Ferry.

Brown and his 18 men quickly overpowered the civilian guards at the Arsenal.

> Open up the Arsenal, or I'll shoot you!

Brown sent parties into the nearby countryside to free the slaves and capture the plantation owners.

We are here to set you free! Seize arms!

No, sir, please not me!

Soon there were 50 captives in the Arsenal. In the morning, the local militia attacked the building.

Steady men. Sell your lives dearly!

A detachment of marines arrived commanded by Colonel Robert E. Lee. When Brown refused to surrender, they battered down the door.

John Brown was captured, convicted of treason, conspiracy, inciting rebellion, and hanged. In the North, moderates like Abraham Lincoln deplored the wild lawlessness of the raid. But the Northern extremists made John Brown into a saint. In the South, after the raid, there were no moderates.

On the day of Brown's execution, mourning services were held in Northern churches.

In the South, it was final proof that they could not remain in the Union.

There, you see? This is proof that the North is in favor of the murderous methods of John Brown.

I'm convinced that the new Republican Party was behind the plot!

Before the election of 1860, Governor Gist of South Carolina wrote to the other Southern governors.

If the Republican nominee, Lincoln, is elected, South Carolina will secede! I am asking the other cotton states what they will do.

In November, Abraham Lincoln was elected president. Quickly South Carolina called a state convention.

It is hereby declared that the Union now subsisting between South Carolina and other states, under the name of the United States of America, is hereby dissolved.

As the news spread, the people of Charleston rushed into the streets to celebrate.

But at sunrise the next morning, at Fort Moultrie across the harbor, the Stars and Stripes was raised as usual.

By February 1861, seven states had seceded from the Union to form the Confederate States of America. In Montgomery, Alabama, Jefferson Davis had become president of the new nation.

The South must make all who oppose us smell Southern powder and feel Southern steel!

The glorious South! In only a month, we've already established a government.

Although Abraham Lincoln was president-elect of the United States, James Buchanan would be in office until March.

And we've seized millions of dollars worth of federal property without a drop of blood to stop us!

Sir, General Twiggs in Texas has turned over 19 army posts to the Southerners!

I have no power to interfere.

Mr. President, the Southerners have seized the New Orleans mint and $300,000 there!

On March 4, the problem became Lincoln's.

I, Abraham Lincoln, do solemnly swear...

I do not believe in secession, but I have no right to compel the seceding states!

Again and again, in his inaugural address, he spoke to the people of the South.

I have no purpose, directly or indirectly, to interfere with ... slavery in the states where it exists. I have no lawful right ... and I have no inclination to do so.

In your hands, my dissatisfied fellow countrymen, and not in mine, is the momentous issue of civil war. The government will not assail you.

Old General Winfield Scott, in command of the United States Army, sent for Colonel Robert E. Lee.

President Lincoln wishes me to ask you to take command of the army.

Sir, I am sorry. I hate slavery and I am opposed to secession, but I could take no part in an invasion of Virginia or the South.

Lincoln called a meeting of his cabinet.

Gentlemen, there is a critical situation in Charleston Harbor.

Major Anderson at Fort Sumter reports his food is almost exhausted. But the Southern authorities refuse to allow him to receive supplies.

Give up the fort!

The Confederacy has seized Federal property all over the South and I have not retaliated. But I will not see Major Anderson starved out of Sumter!

It is not worth fighting over!

Lincoln sent a special messenger to Governor Pickens in Charleston.

I am directed to notify you an attempt will be made to supply Fort Sumter with provisions. No effort will be made to throw in men, arms, or ammunition.

The message was telegraphed to Montgomery, where President Davis called a cabinet meeting.

Has the time come for an attack on Fort Sumter?

Robert Toombs, Confederate secretary of state, was opposed.

It will lose us every friend in the North. You will strike a hornet's nest. It is unnecessary. It puts us in the wrong. It is fatal.

But Davis instructed General Beauregard otherwise.

President Davis instructs me to demand the immediate surrender of Fort Sumter. In case of refusal, we will level the fort!

Major Anderson refused to surrender. On an island in the harbor, Fort Sumter was within easy reach of many Southern guns. At dawn on April 12, 1861, the batteries opened fire. The fighting had begun.

The fort was soon in flames. On the second afternoon, with the walls crumbling, Anderson was forced to surrender.

In the North, crowds gathered outside of newspaper offices waiting for news.

I can't believe it—they fired on Sumter!

What's the latest?

Here comes a bulletin!

No! No!

Now we'll have to whip them!

We'll give old Abe everything he needs!

BULLETIN
SUMTER FALLS!

On April 15, Lincoln issued a proclamation.

Issue a call for 75,000 state militia to serve in the federal army.

Washington itself, capital of the Union, was in danger.

We are surrounded by Virginia, which has seceded, and Maryland, which is about to do so. What have we for defense?

On April 19, he proclaimed a blockade of Confederate ports.

Very little, sir—a few companies of regulars and volunteers, and a handful of marines.

Troops are on their way from Massachusetts and New York, but I am afraid of trouble in Baltimore when they cross town to change trains.

On April 19, the Massachusetts 6th Regiment reached Baltimore and started across the city.

On April 24, Lincoln visited the wounded men of the Massachusetts 6th.

I don't believe there is any North! The 7th Regiment is a myth. You are the only real things.

In Washington the offices and stores were closed, the streets empty.

It is like a city under seige!

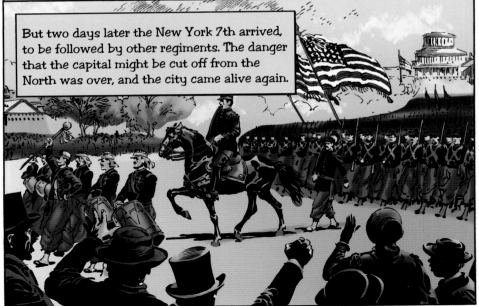

But two days later the New York 7th arrived, to be followed by other regiments. The danger that the capital might be cut off from the North was over, and the city came alive again.

Soon there were troops quartered everywhere in Washington. People expected a short war, quickly won.

What are they waiting for? One easy thrust into Virginia and the Confederacy will collapse!

On to Richmond, that's the idea!

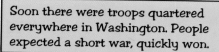

By midsummer, the country was impatient.

Mr. President, we have no army yet, only untrained, inexperienced volunteers!

I know, but the entire North demands an attack!

General Irvin McDowell was in command of the troops around Washington.

On July 16, we will move to attack the main Confederate army under General Beauregard at Manassas.

In two days, the army arrived at a little river known as Bull Run.

The Confederates are dug in on a line beyond the river.

We will attack at early morning.

For a time, things went according to McDowell's plan. The Southern line was pushed back.

But a brigade of Virginia under General T. J. Jackson stood firm.

There is Jackson, standing like a stone wall! Rally behind the Virginians!

Stonewall Jackson had a new name. The Southern troops rallied. Reinforcements arrived.

The day was Sunday. A holiday crowd had driven out from Washington to watch the battle—politicians, socialites, ordinary people by the hundreds.

Oh, Senator, what a thrilling way to picnic!

Yes, indeed! Nice to watch the Johnny Rebs being defeated!

Suddenly there was a charge.

I say—our forces are retreating!

Quick, we must get away!

The Union attack had collapsed. The raw recruits fell back in disorder, but there was no panic until they met the holiday crowd swarming over the highway to Washington. When an overturned wagon blocked a bridge, military and civilian vehicles were hopelessly entangled. It was every man for himself. The soldiers dropped their guns and ran.

The holiday was over. The North knew for the first time that a long, hard war lay ahead.

In 1861, when Lincoln declared a blockade of the Confederate coastline, Southerners laughed.

That Lincoln's a fool! The North has about six old wooden tubs ready for duty!

And we've got 3,500 miles of Atlantic coast, not to mention the Mississippi with even more miles to patrol.

We've got the Norfolk shipyard too, even if the Union troops did burn it when they moved out.

And I hear the Confederate Navy has raised the *Merrimac* that the Yankees sunk and is fixing her up!

The men were right. The Southerners had raised the war ship *Merrimac* and were hard at work.

We're making her into an ironclad. We'll rechristen her the *Virginia* and she'll be invincible.

Word of the rebuilt *Merrimac* reached Lincoln and Naval Secretary Gideon Welles.

We're buying and building ships, increasing our naval strength capacity, but we haven't an ironclad in the lot.

You think the *Merrimac* will be successful?

No wooden ship can stand up to her. We'll never enforce a blockade against the *Merrimac*.

Then we must have ironclads! See to it.

John Ericsson, in New York City, was an inventor. One day he had a visitor.

I'm Cornelius Bushnell. I've come from Washington. Harry Delameter sent me to you.

Yes, come in.

The Union is looking for an ironclad ship. I hear you've developed one. May I see your model?

Yes! I had given up hope. I wrote Washington but I've heard nothing.

You see? It is a floating gun battery. It is impregnable and it will sink anything afloat.

It could save the Union! We must have it.

Given a contract to build it, Ericsson worked night and day to see the ship completed. He was often harassed by doubting navy officers.

I question the stability of such a ship.

Won't the concussion in the turret be too great for men to stay there and fire the gun?

The papers are calling it Ericsson's Folly!

At last the ship went for trials. A navy crew was assembled. A hundred men had volunteered.

Why did I volunteer for this? Guess I wanted to be a hero.

Never saw anything like it! We're heroes just for coming aboard!

At Hampton Roads, across the water from Norfolk Navy Yard where the *Merrimac* was being made ready, five of the Union's best ships were stationed.

Blockade duty! Most boring thing there is!

We sure could use a little action!

It's coming out! A big ship ... the *Merrimac!*

The *Merrimac* was an ugly thing. She plowed through the water toward the sailing vessels. The fire from their guns rattled uselessly against her iron sides. Soon one Union ship was sunk, another afire.

At last, with the tide ebbing, the *Merrimac* pulled away. But everyone knew she would be back the next day.

The news spread rapidly. The next morning, Lincoln and his cabinet waited.

The news is that two of our best ships are sunk, and none of our guns could hurt the *Merrimac*.

We've got to protect Washington. I've ordered barges sunk in the Potomac. The *Merrimac* could steam up and fire on the White House!

The *Monitor* has two guns, I believe! Two guns, against the *Merrimac's* 50!

Mr. Stanton, this is my responsibility! We're trying to keep the Potomac open! The *Monitor* is on her way to Hampton Roads.

Gentlemen, suppose we wait and see what happens!

The *Monitor* arrived at Hampton Roads. From the war ships, they looked down on her.

Cheese box or a raft?

And that's supposed to saves us from the *Merrimac!*

The *Merrimac* arrived, threatening the Union's *Minnesota*. The *Monitor* headed straight for the *Merrimac*.

38

The *Merrimac* fired a broadside into the *Monitor*. It would have crashed through the *Minnesota*.

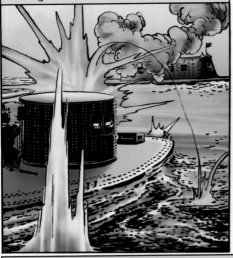

The *Monitor's* turret turned. Two muzzles poked out. Two shots slammed into the *Merrimac*.

When the shots were fired, the guns disappeared and the target revolved offering no target for the *Merrimac* guns.

For three hours the battle raged. Then the *Merrimac* withdrew, limping back into harbor, never to fight again. The navy ordered more *Monitors*. With heavier guns, they could sink anything afloat. It was the end of wooden ships as war ships.

General Robert E. Lee commanded the Confederate Army of Virginia. On September 17, 1862, he was defeated at Antietam. Five days later, Lincoln met with his cabinet.

I made a covenant with God to free the slaves when the rebels were driven from Maryland. This happened at Antietam.

I am therefore issuing an Emancipation Proclamation declaring upon January 1, 1863, all slaves in rebellion states henceforward free.

From the beginning of the war, when Union armies invaded the South, runaway slaves had joined them.

At Fortress Monroe, Virginia, Union General Butler was in command when a Confederate officer arrived under a flag of truce.

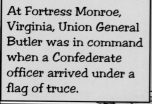

You have three runaway slaves here, sir. They are valuable property. I demand their return.

By withdrawing from the Union, Virginia became foreign territory. I shall detain the blacks as contraband of war.

Camps were later set up for the "contrabands."

After the emancipation, for the first time, black troops were used officially in the Union Army.

Write the governors asking that they recruit black troops. Tell them that the sight of 50,000 armed and drilled black soldiers should end the rebellion.

Frederick Douglass had always urged the use of black troops. Now he became a recruiting officer.

Why should we join up? They won't let us fight with white soldiers.

They pay us less than the whites.

It's your chance to prove yourselves. And it's your fight! Liberty won by white men would lose half its luster.

Massachusetts raised two regiments of black soldiers. Douglass' sons, Charles and Lewis, joined the Massachusetts' 54th under Colonel Robert Shaw.

Fall in, men. We're off for South Carolina.

At Fort Wagner near Charleston, the 54th spearheaded the attack.

I want you to prove yourselves. Move in quick time to within a 100 yards, then double quick and charge!

When they were 200 yards from the fort, the Confederates opened fire. Men fell, but there was no pause.

Sergeant William Carney was the flag bearer. Wounded twice, he still planted the flag on the fort parapet.

For his heroics, Carney won the Congressional Medal of Honor.

On March 3, 1863, the United States passed the first draft law in its history. It was an unfair law and many people did not like it.

Every man between 20 and 45 has to register.

And the only exemptions are for money! Put up $300 and you don't have to go.

Or buy a substitute. Pay somebody to go in your place. You see what that means?

Sure! It's the poor workers who have to fight! And now, to make it worse, we're fighting to free the slaves!

What's wrong with that?

We free 'em and they come up here and work for less money and take our jobs.

In New York on July 13, while the names of draftees were being drawn, a mob drove the provost marshall from his office.

For days rioters roamed the streets, sacking shops and saloons, burning the homes of anti-slavery leaders and blacks, killing several hundred people.

The South was winning more battles than the North, but they had problems too, and also a draft law. In June 1863, with the proportion of deserters reaching one-third of the army, President Davis proclaimed an amnesty for all who would return to the army. Also, the South was running out of supplies.

General Lee decided to invade Pennsylvania.

Our army needs everything—food, shoes, and horses. Soldiers can't fight well hungry and barefoot. Pennsylvania is a rich state.

The prosperous farm country provided horses and food. There were even small shoe factories to raid.

On June 27, Lee and his officers studied a map.

Hereabouts we shall probably meet the enemy and fight a great battle, and if God gives us victory the war will be ended.

Lee's finger rested on the village of Gettysburg.

General Ewell led Lee's 2nd Corps into Gettysburg. He was recovering from an earlier injury and his men took a Yankee carriage for him.

The food in this state is rich and plentiful.

Not knowing where Lee's army was heading, concerned with a threat to Washington, the Union forces moved along roads east of the Confederates. It was by chance the two armies met at the crossroads of Gettysburg.

Have you seen Confederate troops hereabout?

You're Yankees! Thank God! No, no Confederates... not for a few days.

These first Union troops were surprised by the Confederates. They dug in and hoped for reinforcements.

The rebels arrived in greater numbers. The Union reinforcements did not come. Finally the Union troops broke ranks and ran for a nearby rocky ridge.

Perhaps this was the crucial moment of the Battle of Gettysburg. Confederates did not pursue the demoralized Yankees. During the night, Union troops reinforced them. They dug in among the rocks and tombstones of Cemetery Ridge. For three days the battle raged through wheat fields and peach orchards; again and again the rebels charged, but it was Lee who was forced to retreat at last.

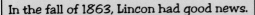

In the fall of 1863, Lincon had good news.

General U. S. Grant has won a big victory at Chattanooga, cutting the South's railroad gateway.

Maybe we've found a general who can win battles! Send for General Grant.

In March 1864, Grant was made commander of all the Union armies. He made plans with General Sherman.

We'll split the Confederacy in two. Take your troops and smash through to Atlanta and the sea. I will attack Lee and capture Richmond.

Fighting through Georgia, Sherman's men burned houses, barns, towns, crops, tore up railroads, leaving a path of destruction 60 miles wide.

I tell you war is hell!

Thousands of freed slaves joined Sherman's march.

On April 2, 1865, the Confederate capital of Richmond fell to Grant's armies. Four days later, Lincoln visited the city.

Thank God I have lived to see it.

On April 9, at the village of Appomattox Court House, Lee surrendered to Grant.

I will have food sent to your armies at once, sir.

Thank you.

Grant dictated a historic message.

General Lee surrendered the Army of Northern Virginia this afternoon.

In Washington, it was Good Friday. Lincoln met with his cabinet.

War creates more problems than it solves. We can't run governments in all the Southern states. Their people must do that, though I reckon at first some may do it badly.

That night, Lincoln went to the theater. During the play John Wilkes Booth stole through the theater to the door of Lincoln's box.

Throwing open the door, Booth shot Lincoln in the head, then jumped to the stage.

A few hours later, Abraham Lincoln was dead.

The following Wednesday, the people of Washington mourned as Lincoln's funeral procession passed by.

People would gather throughout the countryside as the funeral train carried him back to Springfield.

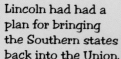

Lincoln had had a plan for bringing the Southern states back into the Union.

Lincoln was right—we should make it easy for the South to come back.

They seceded, didn't they? They fought us all those years! Why should we make it easy for them?

Johnson, the new president, tried to follow Lincoln's plan, but he was opposed by the radical Republicans in Congress, led by Thaddeus Stevens.

I have no use for a reconstruction policy that will turn loose four million slaves without a hut to shelter them or a cent in their pockets!

Stevens favored confiscating Confederate estates and dividing them among former slaves. He also championed black suffrage against those who felt the former slaves were too ignorant to vote.

The ballot is a school master, it teaches manhood. It is especially important to a race whose manhood had been denied.

The differences between Johnson and Congress became so great that Johnson was impeached by the House and tried by the Senate.

Johnson was found not guilty by only one vote. From then on, he had little influence on the course of Reconstruction.

People talked about three important amendments to the Constitution, passed by Congress, and approved by three-fourths of the states.

The 13th Amendment says slavery shall not exist in the United States.

The 14th Amendment says all people born here are citizens and entitled to equal protection under the law.

The 15th says a citizen's right to vote can't be denied him because of race, color, or previous condition of servitude.

Yes, sir, it's easy to remember those amendments if you're black and a former slave!

The Freedmen's Bureau was set up in 1865, growing out of the work carried on by private individuals during the war to help the former slaves. It set up hospitals and schools as well as addressing other problems.

You have a job?

Well, I'm working for my old master.

And does he pay you?

Well no, sir, not very often.

We'll take care of that! You're a free man now and entitled to your wages!

Most important to the former slaves was a chance for an education and the right to vote.

The Abraham Lincoln School for Freedmen was established in New Orleans.

In the elections of 1867–68, many former slaves voted for the first time. Under federal military occupation, 700,000 blacks qualified to vote.

African Americans learned to speak up at electioneering rallies.

Then they went to the polls to cast a vote.

Hiram Revels was the first African American ever to serve in the U. S. Senate.

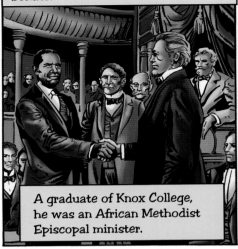

A graduate of Knox College, he was an African Methodist Episcopal minister.

Another Senator representing Mississippi was Blanche K. Bruce, a cotton planter, who also served as sheriff, tax collector, and superintendent of schools.

More than 20 blacks served in the House of Representatives during Reconstruction. And many held state and local offices in the South.

Francis L. Cardoso, educated at the University of Glasgow, was the secretary of state and later treasurer of South Carolina.

Jonathan Gibbs, a graduate of Dartmouth, was secretary of state in Florida and later superintendent of public education.

Frederick Douglass served as a United States marshall.

Many Northerners, both black and white, came South during Reconstruction.

Look at that—another damned carpetbagger arriving!

Among the newcomers were many good people and some rascals. But all were lumped together with the derisive term of "carpetbagger."

Native Southerners trying to make Reconstruction work such as Governor James L. Alcorn of Mississippi, were known as "scalawags."

I propose to vote with the blacks, discuss politics with them, sit in counsel with them, form a platform acceptable to both races, and pluck our common liberty and prosperity from the jaws of inevitable ruin.

The "unreconstructed" white Southerner, unable to regain control politically, resorted to terrorism.

Something's got to be done about these slaves!

I swear, some of them are getting to think they're almost as good as we are!

But what can we do while they're protected by the federal laws and troops?

Let's form a club—dead secret passwords and everything. We'll disguise ourselves and our horses, and go out at night to threaten them.

Count me in!

The big thing is to scare them out of voting!

The idea of the Ku Klux Klan, founded in Pulaski, Tennessee, spread over the South.

You're comin' with us!

The year 1876 was an election year—Hayes against Tilden.

The election was almost a tie. In return for Southern votes, Rutherford B. Hayes promised to withdraw federal troops from the South, and he became president.

During 1877, federal troops were withdrawn from the South. In 1878, an order was passed forbidding the use of federal troops in elections.

PBOEHS PAPERWARE HOUSE

ORLEANS HOTEL

The old abolitionist leaders were gone. The Reconstruction was at an end. Not until 1954 would the Supreme Court give African Americans another chance for equality.